TAKE
ONE

ins

USTER

NGAPORE • TORONTO

Notes for parents and teachers

This book has a theme that threads its way through the subject of the book. It does not aim to deal with the topic comprehensively; rather it aims to provoke thought and discussion. Each page heading makes a simple statement about the illustration which is then amplified and questioned by the text. Material in this book is particularly relevant to the following sections of the National Curriculum for England and Wales:

English: AT2 levels 1–3
Science: AT5 level 1; AT6 level 1, 3; AT9 levels 1–3
Technology: AT1 level 1; AT4 levels 1–3

In Scotland the proposals of the Scottish Education Department apply.

TAKE ONE has been researched and compiled by Simon & Schuster Young Books. We are very grateful for the support and guidance provided by our advisory panel of professional educationalists in the course of the production.

Advisory panel:
Colin Pidgeon, Headteacher
Wheatfields Junior School, St Albans
Deirdre Walker, Deputy headteacher
Wheatfields Junior School, St Albans
Judith Clarke, Headteacher
Grove Infants School, Harpenden

British Library Cataloguing in Publication Data
Baker, Susan
    Mountains.
    1. Mountains
    I. Title. II. Series
    551.432

    ISBN 0–7500–0612–9

Series editor: Daphne Butler
Design: M&M Design Partnership
Photographs: ZEFA
except pp. 17, 18, 21 John Cleare
p. 19 Department of the Environment

First published in Great Britain in 1991 by Simon & Schuster Young Books

Simon & Schuster Young Books
Simon & Schuster Ltd
Wolsey House, Wolsey Road
Hemel Hempstead, Herts HP2 4SS

Printed and bound in Great Britain by BPCC Hazell Books, Paulton and Aylesbury

Contents

Mountain views

Mountains are huge masses of rock that rise up from the valleys and plains. Have you ever seen a high mountain?

Climbing a steep mountain is hard work but it can be fun! Just wait till you see the view!

The last wilderness

The rugged mountain wilderness is a
difficult place for people to reach.
Wild plants, animals and birds
can live there undisturbed.

What wildlife would you look for
in the mountains?

9

Mountain people

People live in some mountain areas.
Why do you think the farmers
keep animals?

The fields may have to be wide steps
cut into the steep hillsides.
They are called terraces.

Mines and quarries

Sometimes you see a huge gash
in a mountainside where people
have dug out stone. What do
they use it for?

What else is mined or quarried
from mountains?

13

How were mountains made?

The Earth's restless crust has slowly
shifted and crumpled, pushing up
huge folds of rock to form mountains.

Rain, wind and water wear rock away.
It turns into sandy grains that end up
in soil or at the bottom of the sea.

15

Snow, ice and glaciers

At the top of the highest mountains
it can be very, very cold.

Snow falls instead of rain.
Water turns to rivers of ice.
Freezing frost makes the rocks
crack and crumble.

Wind and weather

You must be equipped for all weathers when you go into the mountains.
The weather can change suddenly.

Would you enjoy the challenge and adventure of exploring these wild, lonely places?

Mountaineering

People setting out on mountaineering expeditions have to carry everything with them that they need to survive.

Can you think of ten things they should take? How do you think they get water?

Rock climbing

Some mountains have long gentle slopes. Others are steep and rocky. Some climbers choose the hard way to the top!

Climbing can be difficult and dangerous. You need the right equipment and proper training for climbs like these.

23

Snow sports

People enjoy the mountains in summer and winter. They can use special trains, cable cars or lifts for the uphill journey.

Skiers swish downhill over the snow.
What do you like doing in the snow?

26

Mountain railways

Some people like to get to the top under their own steam. Others are pleased to take the train to admire the view from the top.

Mountain railways have special tracks and engines for climbing steep slopes.

Mountain barriers

Long, winding roads and railways have
been built over mountain ranges.
Tunnels have been cut through
some mountains.

Many people fly over the mountains.
How would you like to cross them?

Index